FRUIT CAKES

TASTY BAKES WITH FRESH FRUIT

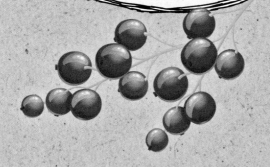

FRUIT CAKES

TASTY BAKES WITH FRESH FRUIT

CONTENTS

Oven temperatures

The oven temperatures in this book are for an electric oven with top and bottom heat. If you are using a fan oven, reduce the temperature by 20 °C. The following table contains the temperature settings for fan and gas ovens:

Top and bottom heat	Fan oven	Gas Mark
140 °C	120 °C	Mark 1
160 °C	140 °C	Mark 2.5
180 °C	160 °C	Mark 4
200 °C	180 °C	Mark 6
220 °C	200 °C	Mark 7

Quantities

Spoon quantities*
1 tbsp flour, baking powder, cornflour = 10 g
1 tbsp chopped nuts = 10 g
1 tbsp ground nuts = 5 g
1 tbsp butter = 10 g
1 tbsp cream = 10 ml
1 tbsp cocoa powder = 5 g
1 tbsp sugar = 15 g
1 tbsp icing sugar = 10 g
1 tbsp jam = 15 g
1 tbsp honey = 15 g
*for 1 slightly heaped tablespoon

Abbreviations

approx. = approximately
cl = centilitre
cm = centimetre
g = gram
kcal = kilocalories
kg = kilogram
kJ = kilojoule
l = litre
ml = millilitre
tbsp = tablespoon
tsp = teaspoon

Others

1 sachet vanilla sugar = 8 g
1 sachet baking powder = 15 g
1 sachet blancmange powder = 35 g

FOREWORD

Whether new to cake-baking or more experienced, a quick tray bake or an impressive berry ganache gateau, Sunday afternoon tea or a big birthday, this book contains recipes that will become firm favourites for any taste and occasion. Moist apple and soured cream tray bake, connoisseurs' yellow plum tray bake with olive oil crumble, sinfully delicious quince tart with champagne sabayon, fresh and fruity Spanish orange cake with pine nuts – the following 100 pages contain these and lots of other fabulous fruit cakes that are just waiting for you to bake them ... and enjoy them.

Happy baking!

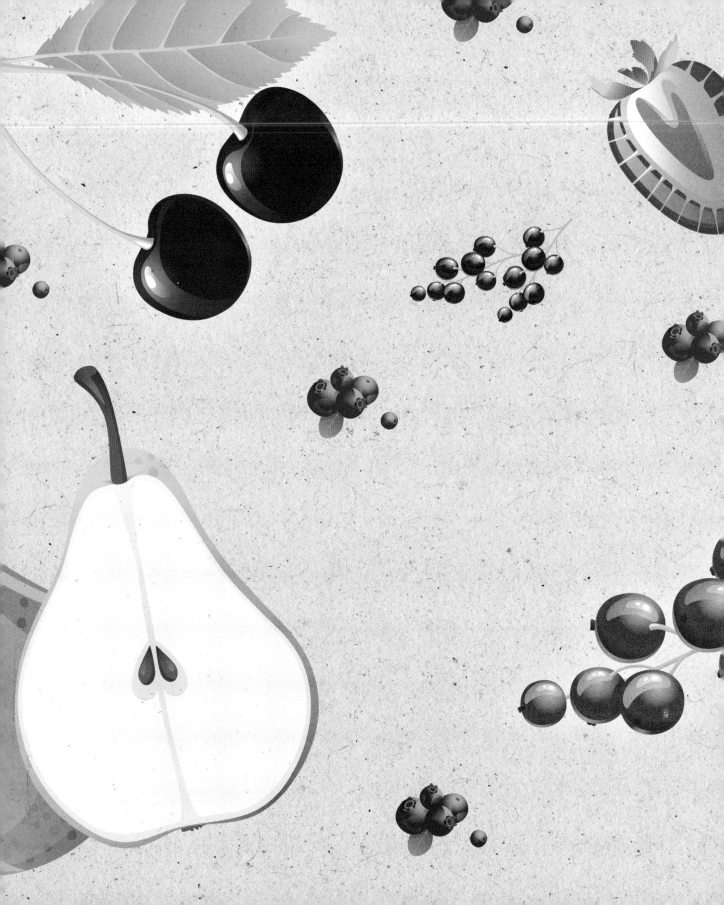

EASY
& GOOD

DELICIOUS FRUIT CAKES
FOR EVERY OCCASION

APPLE AND SOURED CREAM
TRAY BAKE

Makes 20 slices

Sponge mixture:
5 eggs
190 g butter
225 g sugar
pinch of salt
225 g flour

Topping:
1 kg apples
a little lemon juice
500 ml milk
50 g sugar
1 sachet vanilla blancmange
   powder
1 egg
1 egg yolk

Icing:
250 g traditional soured cream
50 g sugar
2 sachets vanilla sugar
3 eggs

Additionally:
butter and breadcrumbs for the tray
sugar to sprinkle

Preparation time:
approx. 50 minutes
(plus baking time)
Per slice: approx. 308 kcal/1290 kJ

Pre-heat the oven to 175 °C (Gas Mark 3.5). Butter a deep baking tray and sprinkle with breadcrumbs. Separate the eggs and whisk the whites until stiff. Chill until required.

To make the sponge mixture, melt the butter in a shallow saucepan and cool slightly. Cream together the egg yolks, sugar and salt. Stir in the flour followed by the melted butter. Fold in the whisked egg whites.

To make the topping, peel and halve the apples, then cut out the cores and slice the flesh. Sprinkle with lemon juice. Make vanilla blancmange from the milk, sugar and blancmange powder in accordance with the packet instructions. Whisk together the egg and egg yolk, and quickly stir into the hot blancmange.

Spread the sponge mixture over the baking tray. Top with the hot blancmange followed by the sliced apples. Stir together the soured cream, sugar, vanilla sugar and eggs. Pour over the apples and bake at the bottom of the oven for 40–45 minutes. Sprinkle the cake with sugar while still hot.

CHOCOLATE AND VANILLA PEAR
CAKE

Makes 12 slices
(springform tin 26 cm diameter)
Vanilla pears:
8 small pears (approx. 800 g)
1 vanilla pod
220 g sugar
1 piece of zest from
    1 non-treated lemon

Sponge mixture:
5 eggs
190 g butter
40 g dark chocolate
    (70 % cocoa)
225 g sugar
pinch of salt
225 g flour
60 g ground almonds

Additionally:
butter and breadcrumbs
    for the tin

Preparation time:
approx. 1 hour
(plus baking time)
Per slice: approx. 467 kcal/1955 kJ

For the vanilla pears, wash, peel and halve them and cut out the cores. Halve the vanilla pod lengthwise and scoop out the pulp.

Put 625 ml water in a saucepan with the vanilla pulp and pod. Add the sugar and lemon zest, and bring to the boil. Put the pears in the liquid and simmer gently over a low heat for about 20 minutes until they are soft. Remove the pears and drain, then boil the syrup until it thickens. Leave to cool.

Pre-heat the oven to 175 °C (Gas Mark 3.5). Butter a springform tin and sprinkle with breadcrumbs. To make the sponge mixture, separate the eggs and whisk the egg whites until stiff. Chill until required.

Melt the butter and chocolate in a shallow saucepan and cool slightly. Cream together the egg yolks, sugar and salt. Combine the flour and ground almonds and stir into the egg yolk mixture. Then stir in the butter and chocolate mixture and 4 tablespoons of pear syrup. Fold in the whisked egg whites.

Put the sponge mixture in the tin and press in the pear halves. Bake the cake in the middle of the oven for about 50 minutes.

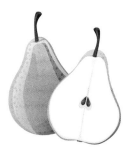

GREENGAGE CAKE
WITH ALMOND LIQUEUR

Makes 16 slices

Sponge mixture:
250 g quark
90 g butter
180 g flour
2 tsp baking powder
3 tbsp sugar
pinch of salt

Topping:
750 g greengages
4 tbsp almond liqueur
2 tbsp icing sugar

Icing:
200 g traditional soured cream
2 eggs
2 tbsp sugar
50 g amarettini

Additionally:
flour for rolling out
icing sugar to dust

Make a sponge mixture from the quark, butter, flour, baking powder, sugar and salt. Knead well, then cover and refrigerate for about 1 hour.

Wash, dry and stone the greengages. Cut the fruits in half, and combine with the almond liqueur and icing sugar.

Pre-heat the oven to 180 °C (Gas Mark 4). Roll the sponge mix out on a floured work surface to the size of a baking tray. Line a baking tray with baking parchment, and place the sponge on top.

To make the icing, whisk together the soured cream, eggs and sugar until fluffy. Crumble the amarettini and sprinkle over the sponge mixture.

Arrange the greengages over the sponge, leaving a margin of about 1.5 cm. Spread the icing over the greengages. Bake the cake in the oven for about 20 minutes. Dust with icing sugar when done. Serve warm.

Preparation time:
approx. 30 minutes
(plus baking and chilling time)
Per slice: approx. 178 kcal/745 kJ

APRICOT AND MARZIPAN
MINI KUGELHOPF CAKES

**Makes 2
(kugelhopf tins,
10 cm diameter each)**

Sponge mixture:
60 g apricots
1 egg
salt
35 g sugar
60 g butter
60 g flour
10 g cornflour
½ tsp baking powder
2 tbsp milk
40 g almond paste

Icing:
60 g icing sugar
1 tsp lemon juice

Additionally:
butter for the tin
chopped pistachios to decorate

Pre-heat the oven to 180 °C (Gas Mark 4). Butter the base and sides of the two tins. Wash and pat dry the apricots and blanche quickly. Skin and chop the flesh.

Separate the egg. Whisk the egg white with a pinch of salt and 15 g of sugar until stiff. Whisk together the butter and the remainder of the sugar until fluffy. Gradually stir in the egg yolks. Combine the flour, cornflour and baking powder, and stir into the sponge mixture, alternating with the milk. Chop and stir in the almond paste. Finally, fold in the whisked egg white in 2 portions.

Spoon half the sponge mixture into each tin. Top with the chopped apricots, then spoon over the remainder of the sponge mixture. Bake the cakes for about 30 minutes. Leave in the tins for a few minutes to cool, then turn out and leave until cold.

To make the icing, combine the icing sugar and lemon juice, plus a little water if required, to make a thick icing. Pour over the kugelhopf cakes, allowing it to run down the sides. Sprinkle over the pistachios. Leave until completely set.

Preparation time:
approx. 40 minutes
(plus baking and cooling time)
Per slice: approx. 690 kcal/2889 kJ

PEAR TART
WITH ROSEMARY

Makes 8 slices

1 sprig rosemary
400 g pears
4 tbsp icing sugar
2 tbsp oil
85 g pine nuts
1 fresh puff pastry round
   (32 cm diameter, from the
   chiller cabinet)

Pre-heat the oven to 220 °C (Gas Mark 7). Rinse and pat dry the rosemary. Brush off the needles, then chop them finely and measure out 1 teaspoon.

Wash and dry the pears, then cut them in half and core. Peel the pears and cut into 1 cm slices.

Caramelise the icing sugar in an ovenproof pan (26–28 cm diameter) until golden. Add the pears, rosemary, oil and pine nuts, and coat all over in the caramel. Remove the pan from the heat.

Arrange the pear slices in the pan in the shape of a star. Place the puff pastry over the contents of the pan and press the sides down. Bake the tart in the oven for 20–25 minutes.

Remove from the oven and leave to cool for a short time. Carefully turn out onto a cake plate before the caramel hardens. Serve the tart warm or cold with whipped cream.

Preparation time:
approx. 25 minutes
(plus baking time)
Per slice: approx. 430 kcal/1820 kJ

YOGHURT AND ALMOND
PLUM CAKE

Makes 20 slices

1 kg plums
1 vanilla pod
6 eggs
300 g sugar
½ tsp salt
120 ml sunflower oil
160 g yoghurt
400 g flour
1 sachet cream of tartar
150 g almond slivers

Additionally:
icing sugar to dust

Pre-heat the oven to 180 °C (Gas Mark 4). Line a deep baking tray with baking parchment. Wash, pat dry and stone the plums. Cut into quarters.

Cut open the vanilla pod lengthways and scoop out the pulp. Whisk together the eggs, 200 g sugar and the salt for about 10 minutes until thick and creamy. Stir together the oil and yoghurt. Combine the flour and cream of tartar, and sift over the cake mixture. Add the oil and yoghurt mixture and the vanilla pulp, and combine well.

Spread the mix over the baking tray and smooth the surface. Arrange the pear quarters on top, and sprinkle over the almond slivers and the remainder of the sugar. Bake the cake in the middle of the oven for about 35 minutes. Remove the cake from the oven and dust with icing sugar before serving.

Preparation time:
approx. 40 minutes
(plus baking time)
Per slice: approx. 280 kcal/1172 kJ

APRICOT AND POPPY SEED CAKE
WITH PISTACHIO CRUMBLE

Makes 12 slices
(springform tin 26 cm diameter)

Sponge mixture and topping:
500 g apricots
1 sachet vanilla sugar
2 tbsp apricot liqueur
150 g butter
5 eggs
50 g sugar
pinch of salt
1 tbsp grated zest of
   1 non-treated lemon
125 g flour
1 tsp baking powder
150 g ground poppy seeds

Crumble topping:
50 g pistachios
150 g flour
big pinch of baking powder
70 g sugar
1 egg yolk
100 g butter

Additionally:
butter and flour for the tin

Wash, dry and halve the apricots and remove the stones. Cut the flesh into slices (not too thin) and put in a bowl. Sprinkle with vanilla sugar and drizzle over the apricot liqueur. Cover and marinate the apricots for about 30 minutes.

Pre-heat the oven to 180 °C (Gas Mark 4). Butter the base and sides of the springform and dust with flour. Melt the butter and allow to cool slightly. Whisk together the eggs, sugar, salt and lemon zest until thick and fluffy. Combine the flour and baking powder, and sift over the top. Add the ground poppy seeds and still-liquid butter. Work into a smooth batter. Spoon into the tin. Arrange the apricots over the top.

To make the crumble, grind or finely chop the pistachios, and knead with all the other ingredients until smooth. Crumble over the cake. Bake in the middle of the oven for about 45 minutes.

Preparation time:
approx. 40 minutes
(plus marinating and baking time)
Per slice: approx. 430 kcal/1800 kJ

CHOCOLATE AND PEACH CAKE
WITH PINE NUTS

Makes 14 slices
(springform tin 26 cm diameter)

500 g peaches
100 g fine dark chocolate
100 g butter
3 eggs
salt
80 g sugar
150 g flour
½ tsp baking powder
100 g pine nuts

Additionally:
butter for the tin
50 g dark chocolate coating
   to decorate
icing sugar to dust

Pre-heat the oven to 180 °C (Gas Mark 4) and butter the inside of the springform tin. Wash, dry and stone the peaches, and chop the flesh into large pieces. Melt the chocolate and butter in a bain-marie.

Separate the eggs. Whisk the egg whites with a pinch of salt until stiff, then chill. Remove the melted chocolate from the hot water. Whisk with the sugar until fluffy, then stir in the egg yolks. Combine the flour and baking powder. Sift over the chocolate, and stir well to combine. Fold in the whisked egg whites and pine nuts in 2 portions.

Put the mixture in the tin. Arrange the peach pieces on top and press down lightly. Bake in the oven for about 45 minutes. Remove from the oven. Leave in the tin for about 15 minutes, then turn out onto a wire rack and leave to cool.

Melt the coating. Drizzle over the cake in thin threads. Leave to set, and dust with icing sugar before serving.

Preparation time:
approx. 40 minutes (plus baking, standing and cooling time)
Per slice: approx. 251 kcal/1051 kJ

QUICK
GRAPE CAKE

Makes 16 slices

700 g seedless grapes
  (green or blue, as preferred)
250 g sugar
200 g butter
4 eggs
2 tbsp semolina
1 sachet vanilla blancmange
  powder
1 kg low-fat quark

Line a baking tray with baking parchment, then pre-heat the oven to 180 °C (Gas Mark 4). Wash, pick over and pat dry the grapes.

Whisk together the sugar and soft butter for about 10 minutes until fluffy, then gradually stir in the eggs, semolina, blancmange powder and low-fat quark.

Spread the quark mixture over the baking tray, then smooth the surface and arrange the grapes evenly on top. Press down lightly, and bake in the oven for about 40 minutes. Cover with a piece of aluminium foil if the cake starts to get too dark.

Preparation time:
approx. 30 minutes
(plus baking time)
Per slice: approx. 276 kcal/1156 kJ

YELLOW PLUM TRAY BAKE
WITH OLIVE OIL CRUMBLE

Makes 24 slices

Base and crumble:
200 g butter
500 g flour
1 tsp baking powder
175 g sugar
½ tsp salt
100 ml fruity olive oil
1 tbsp grated zest of
    1 non-treated orange
1 egg

Topping:
1.2 kg yellow plums
200 g almond paste
75 g sugar
1½ sachets vanilla blancmange
    powder

Additionally:
flour for the work surface
icing sugar to dust

To make the pastry base, cut the butter into small pieces. Combine the flour and baking powder, and sift into a bowl. Add the butter and all the other ingredients for the pastry, and knead together until smooth. Wrap in foil and chill for about 30 minutes.

Pre-heat the oven to 180 °C (Gas Mark 4). Line a baking tray with baking parchment. Wash, dry, halve and stone the yellow plums. Finely chop the almond paste, and combine with the sugar, blancmange powder and plums.

Roll two-thirds of the pastry out onto a floured work surface, then place on the baking tray. Arrange the plum mixture over the top. Crumble over the remainder of the pastry. Bake in the middle of the oven for about 40 minutes. Remove, and dust with icing sugar before serving if desired.

Preparation time:
approx. 45 minutes
(plus baking time)
Per slice: approx. 300 kcal/1256 kJ

PINEAPPLE AND WALNUT CAKE
WITH CARROTS

Makes 8 slices
(loaf tin, 20 cm long)

120 g pineapple (canned)
120 g carrots
50 g walnuts
2 eggs
salt
120 g sugar
1 sachet vanilla sugar
125 g flour
25 g cornflour
½ tsp baking powder
1 tsp baking soda
pinch of cinnamon
40 g grated coconut
100 ml sunflower oil

Additionally:
butter and flour for the tin
150 g icing sugar
1 tbsp pineapple juice
walnut halves to decorate

Pre-heat the oven to 180 °C (Gas Mark 4). Butter the base and sides of the loaf tin and dust with flour. Finely chop the pineapple pieces and place in a sieve to drain until required. Reserve 1 tablespoon of juice for the decoration. Wash, trim, peel and grate the carrots. Chop the walnuts.

Separate the eggs. Whisk the egg whites with a pinch of salt until stiff. Whisk the egg yolks, sugar and vanilla sugar until fluffy. Combine the flour, cornflour, baking powder, baking soda and cinnamon, and sift over. Add the grated coconut. Whisk everything together with the sunflower oil. Stir in the pineapple pieces. Fold in the nuts and carrots. Finally, fold in the whisked egg whites. Pour into the tin and bake in the middle of the oven for about 40 minutes. Remove from the oven and leave in the tin for 10 minutes, then place on a wire rack until cold.

Stir together the icing sugar and pineapple juice until smooth, and spread over the cake. Arrange the walnut halves in a row along the middle of the cake. Leave until set.

Preparation time:
approx. 30 minutes (plus baking, standing and cooling time)
Per slice: approx. 430 kcal/1820 kJ

RHUBARB CAKE
WITH MARZIPAN

Makes 20 slices

Sponge mixture:
200 g almond paste
225 g butter at room temperature
150 g sugar
1 sachet vanilla sugar
pinch of salt
6 eggs
375 g plain flour (patent white)
1 sachet baking powder
3 tbsp milk

Topping:
1.5 kg rhubarb

Additionally:
soft butter and flour for the tray
icing sugar to dust

Butter the baking tray and dust with flour. Pre-heat the oven to 175 °C (Gas Mark 3.5). Wash the rhubarb for the topping, then dry, trim and peel, and cut into pieces about 1.5 cm long.

To make the sponge mixture, first dice the almond paste. Put the butter, sugar, vanilla sugar, salt and almond paste in a mixing bowl and whisk with an electric handheld mixer. Gradually add the eggs and stir in. Combine the flour and baking powder and sift over the egg cream. Stir in quickly with the milk using a wooden spoon.

Spread the mix over the baking tray and smooth the surface. Arrange the rhubarb over the top. Bake the cake in the middle of the oven for about 35 minutes, then remove and leave in the tin until completely cold. Dust with icing sugar before serving.

Preparation time:
approx. 40 minutes
(plus baking and cooling time)
Per slice: approx. 268 kcal/1122 kJ

BLACKBERRY PIE
WITH VANILLA SOURED CREAM

Makes 12 slices
(pie dish 26 cm diameter)

3 sheets frozen puff pastry
1 egg
200 ml cream
2 gelatine leaves
200 g traditional soured cream
1 sachet vanilla sugar
30 g sugar
2 tbsp lemon juice
400 g blackberries

Additionally:
flour for the work surface
soft butter for the tin
icing sugar to dust

Arrange the sheets of puff pastry beside each other on a floured work surface and defrost in accordance with the packet instructions. Butter the tin. Pre-heat the oven to 175 °C (Gas Mark 3.5).

As the pastry is not to rise, quickly knead the sheets together, then roll them out and line the tin. Separate the egg. Stir together 2 tablespoons of the 200 ml of cream for the topping with the egg yolk, and brush over the pastry. Pierce several times with a fork, and bake in the middle of the oven for about 20 minutes until golden. Remove and leave in the tin for about 15 minutes to cool. Place on a wire rack until completely cool.

Soak the gelatine in cold water in accordance with the packet instructions. Stir together the soured cream, vanilla sugar, sugar and lemon juice in a bowl. Squeeze out the gelatine, and melt in 2 tablespoons of water in a saucepan over a low heat. Remove the saucepan from the hob, and stir in 3 tablespoons of the soured cream mixture. Using a wooden spoon, stir this blend into the remainder of the soured cream mixture. Place in the refrigerator for about 20 minutes.

Wash and carefully pat dry the blackberries. Whip the remainder of the cream with an electric handheld mixer until stiff, then use a wooden spoon to fold into the soured cream mixture. Carefully place the puff pastry base on a cake plate, and smooth the soured cream mixture over the top. Arrange the blackberries over the cream, and place in the refrigerator for at least 1 hour before serving. Dust with icing sugar.

Preparation time:
approx. 50 minutes (plus baking, cooling and chilling time)
Per slice: approx. 190 kcal/795 kJ

GOOSEBERRY TRAY BAKE
WITH MERINGUE

Makes 20 slices

1 kg green gooseberries
7 eggs
200 g soft butter
500 g sugar
50 g corn semolina
300 g flour
1 sachet baking powder
100 g ground almonds
salt
1 non-treated lemon
100 g almond paste

Additionally:
butter for the baking frame

Pick over the gooseberries, then wash and carefully pat dry. Separate 5 eggs. Put the egg whites in the refrigerator. Pre-heat the oven to 180 °C (Gas Mark 4). Cover a baking tray with baking parchment and place a buttered baking frame around it. Whisk together the soft butter and 200 g sugar for about 10 minutes until fluffy, then gradually whisk in the 5 egg yolks.

Combine the semolina, flour, baking powder, ground almonds and ½ teaspoon of salt, then add to the butter mixture. Wash the lemon in hot water, then dry. Grate the zest and squeeze out the juice. Add to the butter mixture with the remaining 2 eggs, and whisk until smooth. Spread over the baking tray.

Chop the almond paste and sprinkle over the top. Arrange the gooseberries on top. Bake in the middle of the oven for about 30 minutes. In the meantime, whisk the egg whites with a pinch of salt until stiff. Slowly drizzle in the remainder of the sugar, and continue whisking until you have a firm, glossy meringue mixture.

Remove the cake from the oven. Spoon clouds of meringue over the cake, then bake on the bottom runner of the oven for a further 20 minutes. Remove from the oven. Carefully remove the baking frame, and leave until cold.

Preparation time:
approx. 45 minutes
(plus baking time)
Per slice: approx. 340 kcal/1424 kJ

CHOCOLATEY
BLUEBERRY PIE

Makes 16 slices
(springform tin 26 cm diameter)

300 g blueberries (fresh or frozen)
200 g fine dark chocolate
5 eggs
salt
120 g butter
200 g icing sugar
150 g ground hazelnuts
2 tbsp flour

Additionally:
butter for the tin
icing sugar to dust
whipped cream to serve

Pre-heat the oven to 190 °C (Gas Mark 5) and butter the inside of the springform tin. Wash and dry the blueberries, and remove any remaining stalks. If using frozen berries, allow them to defrost.

Break the chocolate into pieces and melt in a bain-marie. Separate the eggs. Whisk the egg whites with a pinch of salt until they are stiff, then chill. Whisk the soft butter and icing sugar together until fluffy, then gradually stir in the egg yolks.

Stir the hazelnuts, flour and liquid chocolate into the butter and egg yolk mixture, then fold in the whisked egg whites in 2 portions. Pour the mixture into the tin, and arrange two-thirds of the blueberries over the top. Put in the oven and bake for about 40 minutes. After 30 minutes, sprinkle the remainder of the blueberries over the cake.

Leave the cake in the tin to cool, then dust with icing sugar and serve with whipped cream.

Preparation time:
approx. 40 minutes
(plus baking time)
Per slice: approx. 282 kcal/1181 kJ

PEAR AND FOREST FRUIT
STRUDEL

Makes 10 slices

200 g square sheets of filo
    pastry (ready-to-use)
400 g tart pears
2 tbsp lemon juice
1 vanilla pod
1 sachet vanilla blancmange
    powder
500 ml milk
100 g sugar
2 egg yolks
150 g frozen fruits of the forest
2 tbsp cornflour

Additionally:
melted butter to brush
icing sugar to dust

Line a baking tray with baking parchment, then pre-heat the oven to 200 °C (Gas Mark 6). Lay the filo pastry out on a tea towel and brush with a little melted butter.

Peel the pears and pull off the stalks. Cut the flesh into quarters and cut out the cores. Thinly slice the flesh, then blend quickly with the lemon juice. Cut open the vanilla pod and scoop out the pulp.

Prepare the blancmange in accordance with the packet instructions, and stir until cool. Stir in the egg yolks. Combine the defrosted berries with the sliced pears and vanilla pulp. Stir in the cornflour. Combine the fruit mixture with the blancmange, and spread over the filo pastry. Fold the edges of the pastry to the inside, then gently pull the tea towel to roll up in a strudel shape.

Slide the strudel onto the baking tray with the seam on the underside. Brush with melted butter, and bake for about 30 minutes until golden. Add a little more butter if the top starts to look dry. Cool, and dust with icing sugar before serving.

Preparation time:
approx. 30 minutes
(plus baking time)
Per slice: approx. 266 kcal/1114 kJ

QUICK
APRICOT CAKE

Makes 24 slices

250 g flour
240 g sugar
1 heaped tsp baking powder
pinch of salt
250 g soft butter
20 apricots
1 vanilla pod
4 eggs
80 ml milk

Additionally:
butter for the tray
3 tbsp sugar to sprinkle

Pre-heat the oven to 160 °C (Gas Mark 2.5), and butter a baking tray. Sift the flour, sugar, baking powder and a little salt into a bowl, and make a well in the middle. Put the soft butter in this well. Wash, dry, halve and stone the apricots.

Cut open the vanilla pod and scoop out the pulp, then whisk together with the eggs and milk. Pour the egg and milk mixture over the butter, then knead with the flour and sugar for about 3 minutes until smooth.

Pour this mixture onto the baking tray, and smooth over the surface. Arrange the apricots evenly, cut side up, over the cake mixture, and press down lightly. Bake the cake for about 40 minutes, and sprinkle with sugar halfway through the time.

Preparation time:
approx. 30 minutes
(plus baking time)
Per slice: approx. 195 kcal/816 kJ

STRAWBERRY CAKE
WITH COCONUT

Makes 12 slices
(springform tin 26 cm diameter)

Sponge mixture:
100 g butter
80 g sugar
3 eggs
salt
100 g flour
2 tsp baking powder
80 g grated coconut
4 tbsp coconut milk

Topping:
1 kg strawberries
2 sachets cake glaze
80 g sugar

Additionally:
butter for the tin
150 ml cream
50 g icing sugar
50 g grated coconut

Pre-heat the oven to 175 °C (Gas Mark 3.5). Butter the springform tin. Whisk together the butter and sugar until fluffy. Separate the eggs. Gradually stir the egg yolks into the butter mixture. Whisk the egg whites with a pinch of salt until stiff. Combine the flour and baking powder and sift over the butter mixture. Stir in with the grated coconut and coconut milk. Finally, fold in the whisked egg whites, starting with one-third and then the remainder.

Pour into the tin and smooth the surface. Bake in the middle of the oven for about 25 minutes. Remove the cake from the oven and place on a wire rack until cold.

Wash and carefully pat dry the strawberries. Then halve or quarter them, depending on the size. Place the cooled down base on a cake plate and put a cake ring around it. Stir together 1 sachet of cake glaze, 40 g sugar and 250 ml water until smooth. Bring to the boil, then immediately pour over the base. Cover with half the strawberries. Prepare the second sachet of glaze in the same way, and arrange the remainder of the strawberries on top. Chill the cake for 1 hour. To serve, whip the cream and icing sugar until stiff, and fold in the grated coconut. Serve with the cake.

Preparation time:
approx. 45 minutes (plus baking, cooling and chilling time)
Per slice: approx. 320 kcal/1330 kJ

REDCURRANT AND QUARK CRUMBLE

Makes 20 slices

Yeast dough:
125 ml milk
300 g flour
25 g fresh yeast
40 g sugar
40 g butter
pinch of salt
1 egg

Crumble topping:
125 g butter
200 g flour
125 g sugar
pinch of salt
1 egg

Topping:
750 g redcurrants
500 g quark
1 tbsp grated zest of
    1 non-treated lemon
3 eggs
pinch of salt
40 g butter
100 g sugar
1 sachet blancmange powder

Additionally:
flour for the work surface

To make the dough, start by warming the milk. Put 1 tablespoon of flour in a bowl. Crumble in the yeast, and stir in 1 teaspoon of sugar. Pour in a little warm milk. Stir together with a fork, then cover and leave to rise for about 15 minutes.

Melt the butter in the remainder of the milk. Put the remainder of the flour and sugar, the salt and the egg in a bowl. Add the pre-dough and the milk and butter mixture. Knead well until smooth, then cover and leave in a warm place for about 1 hour to rise.

To make the crumble topping, first cut the butter into pieces. Put in a bowl with the flour, sugar, salt and egg, and knead until smooth. Wrap in foil and chill for about 30 minutes.

Pre-heat the oven to 180 °C (Gas Mark 4). Line a baking tray with baking parchment. To make the topping, wash and carefully dry the redcurrants, and strip them from the stalks. Drain the quark. Wash the lemon, then dry and grate 1 tablespoon of zest. Combine the quark and lemon zest. Separate the eggs. Whisk the egg whites and salt until stiff. Whisk the butter and sugar for about 10 minutes until fluffy, then gradually stir in the egg yolks. Sift over the blancmange powder. Add the quark mixture and stir well. Finally, fold in the whisked egg whites.

Knead the dough again, then roll out on a floured work surface and use to line the baking tray. Spread the quark mixture over the top, then sprinkle over the redcurrants. Finish with the crumble topping. Bake in the middle of the oven for about 35 minutes. Remove from the oven and leave to cool.

Preparation time:
approx. 45 minutes (plus rising, baking and cooling time)
Per slice: approx. 250 kcal/1047 kJ

FINE & FANCY

FRUIT CAKES FOR FRIENDS AND FESTIVITIES

CHILLI CHERRY TART
WITH CARAMEL

**Makes 12 slices
(pie dish 24 cm diameter)**

Sponge mixture:
250 g flour
125 g butter
100 g sugar
1 egg
pinch of salt

Topping:
650 g cherries
2 red chilli peppers
150 g sugar
60 g butter
pinch of chilli flakes
2 sachets vanilla sugar

Additionally:
flour for the work surface
crème fraîche to taste

Quickly knead together all the ingredients for the sponge mixture. Wrap in foil and chill for about 1 hour.

To make the topping, wash and pat dry the cherries, then pull off the stalks and pit the fruits. Deseed and wash the chilli peppers and chop into small pieces.

Melt the sugar for the topping in a pan and simmer, stirring, until the caramel starts to turn golden. Then add the butter and chilli peppers, and simmer for about 2 minutes, stirring continuously. The caramel must not turn too dark.

Line the pie dish with baking parchment. Pre-heat the oven to 200 °C (Gas Mark 6). Spread the chilli caramel over the baking parchment, and remove the pieces of chilli. Arrange the cherries over the caramel. Combine the chilli flakes and sugar, and sprinkle over the cherries.

Roll the sponge mix out in a circle on a floured work surface. Drape loosely over the cherries, pressing down firmly on the edge, and pierce several times with a fork. Bake the tart for about 40 minutes, and then immediately turn out on a plate. Serve warm or cold, with a dollop of crème fraîche if desired.

Preparation time:
approx. 45 minutes
(plus chilling and baking time)
Per slice: approx. 340 kcal/1424 kJ

BERRY CHARLOTTE
WITH SPONGE FINGERS

**Makes 12 slices
(springform tin 20 cm diameter)**

Sponge mixture:
2 eggs
75 g butter
90 g sugar
pinch of salt
90 g flour

Filling:
250 g mixed berries
   (e.g. raspberries, blueberries,
   strawberries)
100 ml cream
5 gelatine leaves
270 g quark (20 % fat)
40 g icing sugar
grated zest of ½ non-treated
   orange
2 tbsp orange juice
pulp of 1 vanilla pod

Additionally:
butter and breadcrumbs
   for the tin
approx. 200 g sponge fingers

Pre-heat the oven to 175 °C (Gas Mark 3.5). Butter the small springform tin and sprinkle with breadcrumbs. To make the sponge mixture, separate the eggs and whisk the egg whites until stiff. Chill until required. Melt the butter in a shallow saucepan and cool slightly. Cream together the egg yolks, sugar and salt. Stir in the flour followed by the melted butter. Add the whisked egg whites and fold in.

Put the sponge in the tin and bake in the middle of the oven for about 30 minutes. Leave to cool, then place on a cake plate. Fit a cake ring around it, leaving a small gap. Position the sponge fingers upright along the edge of the cake ring.

To make the filling, wash and pat dry the berries, and cut any large ones in half if necessary. Drain the quark. Whip the cream until stiff. Soak the gelatine in cold water in accordance with the packet instructions, then melt in a saucepan over a low heat, and combine with 2 tablespoons of quark. Stir together the remainder of the quark, icing sugar, orange zest and juice and the vanilla pulp. Gradually stir in the gelatine mixture. Fold in the cream and some of the berries.

Arrange the filling over the base between the sponge fingers. Smooth the surface, and sprinkle over the remainder of the berries. Chill the charlotte for at least 3 hours. Then carefully remove the cake ring and serve the charlotte.

Preparation time:
approx. 1 hour
(plus baking and chilling time)
Per slice: approx. 348 kcal/1457 kJ

PLUM TRAY BAKE
WITH ALMOND BRITTLE

Makes 20 slices

375 g flour
35 g fresh yeast
150 ml milk
200 g sugar
1 egg
pinch of salt
100 g butter
1.25 kg plums
150 g flaked almonds
40 g redcurrant jam

Additionally:
butter for the tray
flour for rolling out

Sift the flour into a bowl. Make a well in the middle and crumble in the yeast. Pour over the warm milk and 1 tablespoon sugar. Stir in 2 tablespoons flour from the edge, then cover and leave in a warm place for 20 minutes to rise.

Add 90 g sugar, the egg, salt and 80 g melted butter to the pre-dough, and knead together until smooth. Cover the dough again and leave in a warm place for 30 minutes to rise.

Roll the dough out onto a floured work surface, then place on a greased baking tray. Cover and leave to rise for about 30 minutes.

Pre-heat the oven to 200 °C (Gas Mark 6). Wash, dry and halve the plums and remove the stones. Caramelise the remainder of the sugar in a pan with the remainder of the butter and the almonds. Put the caramel on the buttered surface. Leave to cool, then chop into pieces.

Arrange the plums over the dough, and bake in the oven for about 35 – 40 minutes. Warm the jam and brush over the cake. Sprinkle the brittle over the plum cake.

Preparation time:
approx. 45 minutes
(plus rising and baking time)
Per slice: approx. 235 kcal/984 kJ

MANGO KUGELHOPF
WITH CARAMEL SPLINTERS

**Makes 16 slices
(kugelhopf tin of 2 l content)**

Sponge mixture:
2 mangoes
5 eggs
pinch of salt
250 g sugar
150 g full-fat quark
350 g flour
2 tsp baking powder

Caramel splinters:
75 g sugar

Additionally:
butter and flour for the tin
250 ml cream
1 sachet vanilla sugar

Pre-heat the oven to 180 °C (Gas Mark 4). Brush the tin with butter and dust with flour. Peel the mangoes and cut the flesh away from the stones. Weigh out 200 g of flesh, and cut into small cubes about ½ cm long.

Separate the eggs. Whisk the egg whites with salt, drizzle in 50 g sugar and continue whisking until the sugar crystals have dissolved and the whites are very stiff. Chill until ready to continue.

Whisk the egg yolks with the remainder of the sugar until pale yellow, thick and creamy. Stir in the quark. Combine the flour and baking powder, then sift over the egg yolk mixture and stir in. Finally, fold in the diced mango and whisked egg whites.

Put the mixture in the tin, and bake on the second runner from the bottom for 50–60 minutes. Insert a wooden cocktail stick in the cake to see if it is done, and remove from the oven when it is. Leave in the tin for about 10 minutes, then turn out onto a wire rack and leave until cold.

To make the caramel splinters, heat the sugar and 2 tablespoons of water in a saucepan, stirring continuously, and boil to make a golden caramel. Pour onto baking parchment, and spread out as thinly as possible. Leave until cold and hard, then run over with a rolling pin to break the caramel into small splinters. Whisk the cream and vanilla sugar until stiff. Serve the kugelhopf with cream and caramel splinters.

Preparation time:
approx. 50 minutes
(plus baking and cooling time)
Per slice: approx. 253 kcal/1059 kJ

EXTRA MOIST
WHITE WINE AND APPLE CAKE

Makes 14 slices
(springform tin 26 cm diameter)

100 g butter
200 g brown sugar
3 eggs
350 g flour
1 sachet baking powder
125 ml milk
125 ml white wine
1 kg tart apples

Additionally:
butter and flour for the tin

Pre-heat the oven to 190 °C (Gas Mark 5), then butter the tin and dust with flour.

Whisk the soft butter and the sugar for about 15 minutes until fluffy, then gradually stir in the eggs. Sift over the flour and baking powder and pour over the milk and white wine, then stir until smooth.

Peel and core the apples and chop the flesh into small pieces. Fold into the cake mixture. Put the cake mixture in the tin and bake for about 45 minutes.

Preparation time:
approx. 30 minutes
(plus baking time)
Per slice: approx. 266 kcal/1114 kJ

FRUITY QUINCE TART
WITH CHAMPAGNE SABAYON

Makes 12 slices
(pie dish 28 cm diameter)
Sponge mixture:
100 g butter
200 g flour
1 egg
60 g sugar
pinch of salt

Topping:
80 g white chocolate
1 kg quince
300 ml white wine
100 g sugar
2 tsp grated zest of
   1 non-treated lemon
5 leaves white gelatine

Sabayon:
200 ml champagne
60 g sugar
4 egg yolks
1 tsp lemon juice

Additionally:
flour for the work surface
butter for the tin
dried legumes to bake blind
12 walnut halves to decorate
3 tbsp quince jelly to brush

Preparation time:
approx. 50 minutes
(plus baking and chilling time)
Per slice: approx. 320 kcal/1340 kJ

Quickly combine all the ingredients for the sponge mixture. Shape into a ball, then wrap in foil and chill for about 1 hour.

Pre-heat the oven to 200 °C (Gas Mark 6). Roll the sponge out on a floured work surface and use to line the buttered pie dish. Pierce the base several times with a fork. Place a piece of baking parchment over the sponge mixture, and weigh it down with dried legumes. Bake in the middle of the oven for about 15 minutes. Remove from the oven. Lift off the dried legumes and parchment, and bake the sponge for about 5 more minutes. Remove from the oven and leave to cool.

To make the topping, chop the white chocolate. Melt in a bain-marie, and brush over the sponge base. Wash, dry and peel the quince and cut out the cores. Chop the flesh. Put in a saucepan with the white wine, sugar and lemon zest, and simmer for about 40 minutes until soft. Then purée in the liquid. Soak the gelatine in cold water in accordance with the packet instructions. Squeeze out, and dissolve in the still-hot quince purée. Leave the purée to cool, then spread over the base. Arrange the 12 walnut halves in a circle over the tart. Heat the quince jelly until liquid and glaze the tart. Cover, and refrigerate for at least 3 hours until set.

To make the sabayon, just before serving whisk all the ingredients in a bain-marie until thick and creamy. Serve with the quince tart.

APRICOT TART
WITH WHITE CHOCOLATE SAUCE

**Makes 12 slices
(hobproof pie dish or
ovenproof pan 28 cm diameter)**

600 g apricots
3 sheets frozen puff pastry
100 g sugar
100 ml orange juice
1 tsp grated zest of
   1 non-treated orange
1 tsp grated zest of
   1 non-treated lemon
2 tbsp butter

Chocolate sauce:
200 ml cream
125 g white chocolate
pinch of salt

Additionally:
flour for the work surface

Wash the apricots. Blanche briefly in boiling water, then drain in a sieve and skin. Halve and remove the stones.

Pre-heat the oven to 180 °C (Gas Mark 4). Defrost the puff pastry. Caramelise the sugar in a hobproof pie dish or ovenproof pan until golden. Deglaze with orange juice, then stir in the grated orange and lemon zest and butter. Simmer until you have a syrup.

Arrange the apricot halves in the pan or pie dish with the rounded sides down. Roll the puff pastry out onto a floured work surface, then roll out lightly and place over the apricots. Press down well on the edges.

Bake in the pre-heated oven for about 30 minutes. Place a cake plate on top, and carefully turn the tart over.

While the pie is baking, make the chocolate sauce. Heat the cream and chop the chocolate. Add to the cream with a pinch of salt and melt. Cool slightly, then whisk until fluffy. Arrange on plates with the tart.

Preparation time:
approx. 30 minutes
(plus baking time)
Per slice: approx. 250 kcal/1047 kJ

CRUNCHY
STRAWBERRY GATEAU

Makes 12 slices
(springform tin 26 cm diameter)

250 g white chocolate coating
270 ml cream
100 g cornflakes
100 g flaked almonds
750 g strawberries
1 sachet whipping cream
   thickening agent
1 sachet vanilla sugar

Decoration:
70 g white chocolate
12 pretty strawberries,
   leaves attached
chopped pistachios to sprinkle

Line the springform tin with baking parchment. Melt the coating with 2 tablespoons cream in a bain-marie, then combine with the cornflakes and flaked almonds. Arrange over the springform base and press down.

Whip the remainder of the cream with the thickening agent and vanilla sugar until stiff. Smooth half the vanilla cream over the chocolate and almond base. Wash, pat dry and hull the 750 g strawberries, then halve them and arrange over the cream layer. Arrange the remainder of the vanilla cream over the strawberries and smooth.

Wash and carefully pat dry the 12 strawberries for the decoration. Do not hull, and do not cut in half. Melt the white chocolate in a bain-marie. Dip one half of the strawberries for the decoration in the chocolate, and arrange on the gateau. To finish, sprinkle a few chopped pistachios over the middle strawberry. Chill until ready to serve.

Preparation time:
approx. 30 minutes
Per slice: approx. 332 kcal/1390 kJ

CHERRY AND QUARK CAKE

Makes 12 slices
(springform tin 26 cm diameter)

Sponge mixture:
6 eggs
50 g flaked almonds
200 g sugar
100 g flour
100 g cornflour
25 g vanilla blancmange powder
1 tsp baking powder
50 g almond paste

Fillings:
750 g sour cherries from a jar
1 sachet red cake glaze
60 g sugar
250 g quark
1 sachet custard powder
  (no cooking required)
pulp of 1 vanilla pod
250 ml cream

Decoration:
12 cocktail cherries
150 ml cream

Preparation time:
approx. 1 hour
(plus cooling and chilling time)
Per slice: approx. 278 kcal/1164 kJ

To make the sponge, first separate the eggs. Dry-fry the flaked almonds in a pan. Whisk the egg whites until stiff, then drizzle in 200 g sugar and whisk until smooth and glossy. Carefully stir in the egg yolks. Combine the flour, cornflour, flaked almonds, blancmange powder and baking powder, and dust over the egg whites. Crumble the almond paste and likewise sprinkle over the egg whites. Carefully fold to combine.

Line a springform tin with baking parchment, and put the sponge mixture inside. Bake in the pre-heated oven at 200 °C (Gas Mark 6) on the second runner from the bottom for about 30 minutes, then leave to cool. When cold, carefully remove the cake from the tin and slice horizontally 3 times (4 layers).

Drain the cherries, reserving the juice. Make a glaze from the cake glaze, 30 g sugar and about 250 ml cherry juice in accordance with the packet instructions. Fold in the cherries, then leave until cool but not set.

Stir together the quark, custard powder, vanilla pulp and the remainder of the sugar. Whip the cream until stiff, and fold in.

Place one cake layer on a cake plate with a suitable springform ring around it. Spread half the cherry mixture over this layer, then top with the second layer, and spread over half the quark mixture. Place the third layer on top, then the remainder of the cherries, and finish with the final layer.

From the remainder of the quark mixture, pipe 12 blobs onto the cake, and top each one with a cocktail cherry. Place in the refrigerator for 2 hours. To serve, whip 150 ml cream until stiff, and spread around the edge.

FOREST FRUIT GANACHE GATEAU

Makes 8 slices
(springform tin 18 cm diameter)

Sponge base:
20 g butter
2 eggs
pinch of salt
60 g sugar
70 g flour
1 tbsp cocoa powder

Topping:
200 g fine dark chocolate
300 ml cream
200 g mixed berries
   (fresh or frozen)
2 tbsp blackcurrant jam
½ sachet cake glaze
125 ml cherry juice
1 tbsp icing sugar

Additionally:
butter and flour for the tin
50 g grated chocolate

Pre-heat the oven to 180 °C (Gas Mark 4), then butter the tin and dust with flour. Melt the butter in a small saucepan, then remove from the heat. Separate the eggs.

Whisk the egg whites with a pinch of salt until stiff. Whisk the egg yolks and sugar until light and fluffy. Combine the flour and cocoa powder, and sift over. Add the just-liquid butter. Fold in the whisked egg whites in 2 portions, and carefully combine. Pour into the tin and smooth the surface. Bake in the middle of the oven for about 25 minutes. Remove from the oven, then take out of the tin and place on a wire rack to cool.

To make the topping, chop the dark chocolate. Heat the cream. Remove the pan from the hob. Pour in the chocolate and leave to stand for about 5 minutes, then stir to combine. Leave to cool to room temperature, and chill for at least 2 hours.

Wash and carefully pat dry fresh fruits, or defrost if using frozen fruit. Halve the chocolate sponge horizontally. Place the bottom layer on a cake plate with a cake ring around it. Warm the blackcurrant jam until liquid, then spread over the cake base.

Whisk the chocolate mixture until stiff. Spread slightly less than half of it over the cake layer. Place the second layer on top. Again, spread with chocolate cream, but reserve a little for the sides. Top with the fruit.

Prepare the cake glaze in accordance with the packet instructions, using cherry juice and icing sugar. Pour over the fruit. Chill the cake until the glaze has set. Loosen the cake ring. Spread the remainder of the chocolate cream over the sides, and cover with grated chocolate.

Preparation time:
approx. 40 minutes
(plus baking and chilling time)
Per slice: approx. 400 kcal/1700 kJ

CHOCOLATE AND RASPBERRY
LAYER CAKE

Makes 16 slices
(springform tin 20 cm diameter)

Sponge mixture:
6 eggs
320 g sugar
80 g flour
2 sachets chocolate blancmange
   powder
2 tsp baking powder

Filling:
350 g raspberries (or mixed berries)
8 leaves white gelatine
600 g low-fat yoghurt
250 g mascarpone
juice and grated zest of 1 lime

Additionally:
cocoa powder and icing sugar
   to dust

Pre-heat the oven to 175 °C (Gas Mark 3.5). Separate the eggs. Whisk the egg whites with 2 tablespoons cold water until they are stiff. Drizzle in 100 g sugar, stirring continuously, and continue whisking until the sugar has dissolved. Stir in the egg yolks. Combine the flour, blancmange powder and baking powder, and carefully fold in.

Spread the mixture over the base in the parchment-lined springform tin. Bake in the oven for 30–40 minutes. Turn the cake out of the tin. Remove the baking parchment, and leave the cake to cool.

Pick over the raspberries, then wash and drain. Soften the gelatine in accordance with the packet instructions. Combine the remainder of the sugar with the yoghurt, mascarpone, lime juice and zest. Squeeze out the gelatine and dissolve in a little liquid, then combine with a little of the yoghurt cream. Fold into the yoghurt cream.

Set aside one-third of the cream, and stir 250 g raspberries into the remaining two-thirds. Once cool, cut the base in half horizontally, twice. Put one layer on a cake plate with a cake ring around it. Spread half the raspberry cream over the base. Place a second layer on top, and spread over the remainder of the raspberry cream. Top with the third layer, and spread over the yoghurt cream without berries. Arrange the remainder of the raspberries in the middle of the cake. Place in the refrigerator for about 5 hours until set. Loosen the cake ring. Dust the cake with cocoa powder and icing sugar.

Preparation time:
approx. 40 minutes
(plus baking and chilling time)
Per slice: approx. 245 kcal/1026 kJ

BADEN PLUM GATEAU

Makes 12 slices
(springform tin 24 cm diameter)
Sponge mixture:
6 eggs
1 vanilla pod
salt
100 g icing sugar
1 tbsp rum
40 g breadcrumbs
150 g ground hazelnuts

Topping:
1 kg damsons or plums
150 g sugar
1 cinnamon stick
1 vanilla pod
1 clove
30 g cornflour
4 leaves white gelatine
500 ml cream
2 sachets vanilla sugar
100 g flaked almonds

Additionally:
butter for the tin

Separate the eggs. Cut open the vanilla pod and scoop out the pulp. Butter the base and sides of the springform tin. Pre-heat the oven to 180 °C (Gas Mark 4).

Whisk the egg whites with a pinch of salt until stiff, then chill. Whisk together the egg yolks, icing sugar and vanilla pulp until pale yellow, then stir in the rum. Sprinkle over the breadcrumbs and hazelnuts and stir in, followed by the whisked egg whites in 2 batches. Put the cake mixture into the springform tin and bake for 35 minutes. Remove, then leave to cool and cut in half horizontally.

Wash, dry, halve and stone the plums. Reserve 12 plum quarters as decoration. Put in a saucepan with 250 ml water, the sugar, cinnamon stick, scooped vanilla pulp and the clove, and cook for about 10 minutes. Put the plums in a sieve and remove the spices. Save the juice and return to the saucepan. Stir the cornflour into 1 tablespoon of water until smooth, then add to the juice and bring to the boil. Leave to cool.

Soften the gelatine in accordance with the packet instructions. Measure out 2 tablespoons of cream, and whisk the remainder with the vanilla sugar. Heat the 2 tablespoons of cream and dissolve the squeezed-out gelatine in it. Stir into a small amount of whipped cream, then combine with the rest.

Spread the thickened juice over the bottom layer and top with the plums. Smooth half the cream over the plums, then cover with the other cake half. Spread the remainder of the cream over the gateau. Garnish the sides with flaked almonds and the top with the reserved plum quarters. Chill until ready to serve.

Preparation time:
approx. 40 minutes
(plus cooking and baking time)
Per slice: approx. 450 kcal/1884 kJ

STRAWBERRY SNAKE
FOR THE KIDS!

Makes 1 snake (about 16 slices)

Sponge mixture:
500 g flour
3 tsp baking powder
100 g sugar
½ tsp salt
150 g butter
2 eggs
200 ml cream

Filling and topping:
700 g strawberries
125 g sugar
400 ml cream
2 sachets whipping cream
  thickening agent
2 sachets vanilla sugar

Additionally:
2 chocolate dots (for the eyes)

Pre-heat the oven to 200 °C (Gas Mark 6). Line a baking tray with baking parchment. Combine the flour and baking powder, and sift into a bowl. Add the sugar and salt. Stir in the butter in flakes. Whisk together the eggs and cream, and pour over. Now knead everything together quickly with your hands, just until you have a smooth sponge mix.

Shape into a roll (about 3 cm diameter), and wind onto the prepared baking tray as shown. Press down gently to flatten slightly. Bake in the middle of the oven for about 15 minutes until golden. Remove from the oven and leave to cool.

Wash, dry and hull the strawberries (set aside 1 large piece of green for the tongue), and slice the fruits. Combine with sugar, then cover and leave to stand for about 30 minutes.

Cut in half lengthways and place on a suitable plate. Whisk together the cream, thickening agent and vanilla sugar until stiff. Arrange strawberry slices over the bottom half. Top with a little whipped cream. Place the second layer of the "snake" on top, and continue in the reverse order, i.e. spread over a little cream, and then arrange the slices of strawberry to look like scales.

To make the eyes, dot on 2 little blobs of cream, and place a chocolate dot on each one. Cut a strip off the reserved piece of green, and insert in the slot as the tongue.

Preparation time:
approx. 30 minutes
(plus baking and standing time)
Per slice: approx. 375 kcal/1570 kJ

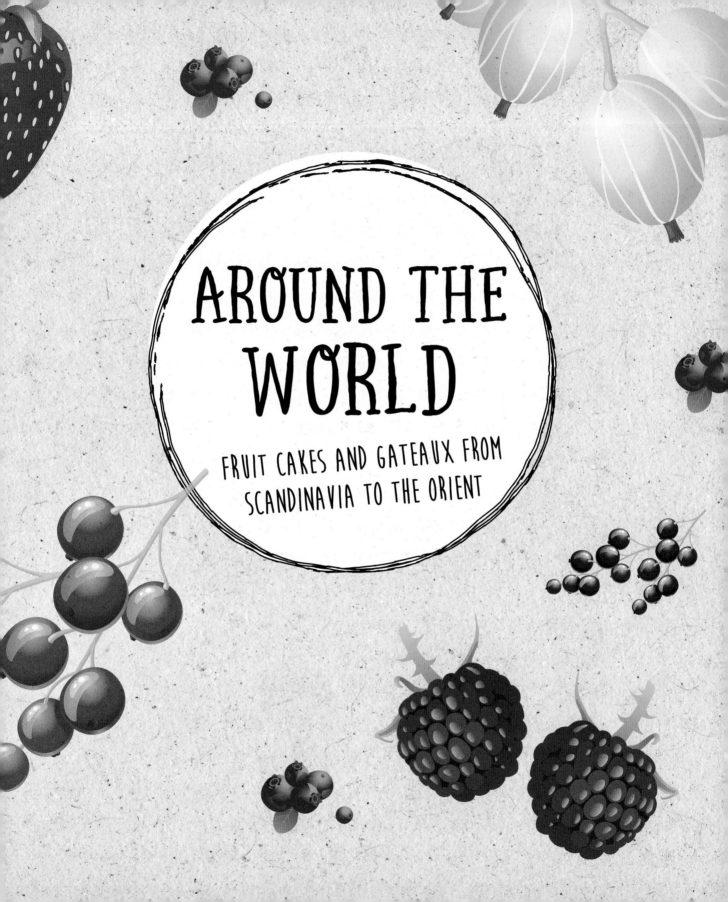

AROUND THE WORLD

FRUIT CAKES AND GATEAUX FROM SCANDINAVIA TO THE ORIENT

SWEDISH
APPLE CAKE

Makes 20 slices

Sponge mixture:
5 eggs
190 g butter
1 vanilla pod
225 g sugar
pinch of salt
225 g flour

Topping:
1.5 kg tart apples
5 tbsp sugar
2 tsp cinnamon

Additionally:
butter and breadcrumbs
    for the tray

Pre-heat the oven to 175 °C (Gas Mark 3.5). Butter a baking tray and sprinkle with breadcrumbs. Separate the eggs and whisk the whites until stiff. Chill until required.

Melt the butter in a shallow saucepan and cool slightly. Halve the vanilla pod lengthwise and scoop out the pulp. Cream together the egg yolks, sugar, vanilla pulp and salt. Stir in the flour followed by the melted butter. Fold in the whisked egg whites.

To make the topping, wash and peel the apples, then cut out the cores and slice the flesh. Spread the cake mixture over the baking tray and arrange the apple pieces on top like roof tiles. Combine the sugar and cinnamon, and sprinkle evenly over the top. Bake the apple cake in the middle of the oven for 35–45 minutes.

Preparation time:
approx. 35 minutes
(plus baking time)
Per slice: approx. 233 kcal/976 kJ

SPANISH
ORANGE CAKE

Makes 12 slices
(springform tin 26 cm diameter)

Sponge mixture:
3 non-treated oranges
5 eggs
190 g butter
225 g sugar
5 drops almond flavour
pinch of salt
225 g flour
150 g ground almonds

Soaking:
4 tbsp orange liqueur

Topping:
50 g almond slivers
400 ml cream

Preparation time:
approx. 45 minutes
(plus baking time)
Per slice: approx. 705 kcal/2952 kJ

Pre-heat the oven to 190 °C (Gas Mark 5). Line the base of a springform tin with baking parchment. For the cake mixture, wash the oranges in hot water, then dry and finely pare the zest from 2 oranges. Using a zester, take long, thin strips from the third orange, and set aside to use as garnish. Squeeze out 1 orange.

Separate the eggs and whisk the whites until stiff. Chill until required. Melt the butter in a shallow saucepan and cool slightly.

Cream together the egg yolks, sugar, bitter almond flavour, 2 tablespoons orange juice, orange zest and salt. Stir in the flour and ground almonds, followed by the liquid butter. Fold in the whisked egg whites.

Put the cake mixture in the tin and bake in the middle of the oven for about 50 minutes. Carefully remove the cake from the tin and turn out onto a wire rack. Remove the baking parchment, and turn the cake over. Stir together the remainder of the orange juice and the orange liqueur, and pour over the cake while still hot. Leave the cake until quite cold.

In the meantime, to make the topping, dry-fry the almond slivers in a pan until golden, then leave to cool. Whisk the cream until stiff. Put the cake on a cake plate and brush with the cream. Sprinkle over the almond slivers and orange zests.

FRENCH
PEAR TART

Makes 8 slices
(pie dish 26 cm diameter)

Sponge mixture:
150 g plain flour (patent white)
80 g cold butter
50 g sugar
pinch of salt
1 egg yolk

Topping:
3 ripe pears (each approx. 200 g)
2 tbsp lemon juice
2 tbsp pear brandy
1 tbsp sugar
pinch of ground allspice

Icing:
125 ml cream
2 egg yolks
2 sachets vanilla sugar

Additionally:
soft butter for the tin
flour for the work surface
icing sugar to dust

To make the sponge mixture, sift the flour into a bowl and dot flakes of butter on top. Add the sugar, salt and egg yolk. Quickly knead together with your hands to make a smooth sponge mix. Work in 1 tablespoon of water if it is too dry. Roll the sponge into a ball and wrap in clingfilm. Chill in the refrigerator for at least 30 minutes.

For the topping, wash and dry the pears, then peel them and cut into quarters. Remove the cores and cut the flesh into thin slices. Combine in a bowl with lemon juice, pear brandy, sugar and allspice.

Pre-heat the oven to 220 °C (Gas Mark 7). Butter the pie dish. Roll the pastry out to the size of the pie dish. Press into the tin, shaping a small rim around the side. Pierce several times with a fork. Arrange the pears on the pastry so they overlap. Bake the tart on the bottom runner for about 30 minutes.

To make the icing, whisk together the cream, egg yolk and vanilla sugar using an electric handheld mixer. Pour over the pears when they have been baking for 10 minutes. Once the icing has set, remove the tart from the oven and leave to cool for a few moments. Best served warm, dusted with icing sugar.

Preparation time:
approx. 50 minutes (plus chilling, baking and cooling time)
Per slice: approx. 200 kcal/837 kJ

BLACKCURRANT
CLAFOUTIS

Serves 14
(pie dish 26 cm diameter)

500 g blackcurrants
1 vanilla pod
3 eggs
120 g sugar
salt
100 ml milk
4 tbsp flour
1 tsp baking powder
100 g ground hazelnuts

Additionally:
butter for the tin
crème fraîche to taste

Pre-heat the oven to 220 °C (Gas Mark 7) and butter the pie dish. Wash and pat dry the blackcurrants, and remove the stalks. Cut open the vanilla pod with a knife and scoop out the pulp.

Whisk together the eggs, the sugar, a pinch of salt and the vanilla pulp until fluffy. Stir in the milk. Combine the flour and baking powder, and fold in with the hazelnuts.

Arrange the blackcurrants over the bottom of the dish and pour over the cake mixture. Bake in the oven for about 35 minutes, then leave in the dish to cool. The dafoutis may be served while still warm with a dollop of crème fraîche.

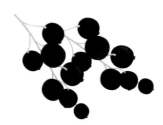

Preparation time:
approx. 30 minutes
(plus baking and cooling time)
Per portion: approx. 171 kcal/716 kJ

TARTE
AU CITRON

Makes 8 slices
(pie dish 22 cm diameter)

150 g flour
150 g butter
pinch of salt
4 gelatine leaves
juice and grated zest of
    3 non-treated lemons
3 eggs
150 g sugar

Additionally:
butter for the dish
flour for rolling out
1 bag baking beans to bake blind
1 non-treated lemon to decorate

Make a shortcrust pastry from the flour, 75 g butter, salt and 1 table-spoon cold water, and knead well. Wrap in foil and chill for 30 minutes.

Pre-heat the oven to 220 °C (Gas Mark 7). Butter the pie dish. Roll out the pastry and place in the dish. Place baking parchment on top, and weigh down with baking beans. Bake blind for about 15 minutes. Remove the baking beans and paper, and leave the pastry to cool.

Soak the gelatine in cold water. Whisk the eggs and sugar until fluffy. Stir in the lemon juice and zest, followed by the remainder of the butter. Heat in a bain-marie until thick, stirring continuously. Dissolve the squeezed-out gelatine in this mixture, then simmer for about 2 minutes and remove from the hob.

Pour the cream over the pastry and place in the refrigerator to set. Wash the lemon in hot water and cut into very thin slices. Arrange decoratively over the tart.

Preparation time:
approx. 30 minutes (plus chilling, baking and cooling time)
Per slice: approx. 348 kcal/1457 kJ

CLASSIC
TARTE TATIN

Makes 12 slices
(pie dish 26 cm diameter)

Sponge mixture:
220 g plain flour (patent white)
130 g cold butter
40 g sugar
pinch of salt
1 egg

Topping:
40 g butter
1 kg apples
1 tbsp lemon juice
80 g sugar

Additionally:
soft butter for the tin
flour for the work surface
200 ml cold cream
2 sachets vanilla sugar

Preparation time:
approx. 50 minutes
(plus chilling and baking time)
Per slice: approx. 316 kcal/1323 kJ

To make the sponge mixture, sift the flour into a bowl and dot flakes of butter on top. Add the sugar, salt and egg, and knead quickly with your hands to make a smooth spone mixture. Roll into a ball. Wrap in cling-film and place in the refrigerator for at least 30 minutes.

To make the topping, melt the butter in a small saucepan without letting it turn brown. Wash and wipe dry the apples, then peel, quarter and core. Slice lengthways, then combine with the lemon juice in a bowl.

Heat the sugar and 50 ml water in a pan. Caramelise, stirring continuously, until golden. Add the apple slices and butter to the caramel. Sauté the apples over a medium heat for about 5 minutes, stirring occasionally.

Pre-heat the oven to 200 °C (Gas Mark 6). Butter the pie dish, and place the apple and caramel mixture inside. Roll the sponge out in a circle the size of the pie dish on a floured work surface. Place over the apple mixture, pressing down well around the edge. Pierce the top several times with a fork. Bake the tart in the middle of the oven for about 30–35 minutes until the top is just golden.

Remove the tart from the oven, and carefully run a sharp knife between the sponge and the dish to loosen it. Turn the hot tart out onto a cake plate. Whip the cold cream and vanilla sugar until stiff, and serve with the warm tarte tatin.

LINZER SCHNITTEN
FROM AUSTRIA

Makes 20 slices

Sponge mixture:
450 g butter
500 g flour
200 g sugar
2 eggs
2 egg yolks
500 g ground hazelnuts
1 tsp cinnamon
grated zest of ½ non-treated lemon

Topping:
400 g raspberry jam

Additionally:
flour for the work surface

Cut the butter into small pieces and put in a bowl with the flour. Add the sugar, 1 egg, both egg yolks, the ground hazelnuts, cinnamon and lemon zest, and knead together to make a smooth sponge mixture. Wrap in foil and place in the refrigerator for at least 1 hour.

Pre-heat the oven to 180 °C (Gas Mark 4). Line a baking tray with baking parchment. Roll two-thirds of the sponge mixture out on a floured work surface until just a little larger than the baking tray. Line the tray with the mixture, and shape a small rim around the edges.

Spread the raspberry jam over the pastry. Roll out the remainder of the pastry and use a pastry wheel to cut into strips. Arrange in a grid over the jam, pressing down firmly on the edges. Beat the second egg and brush over the pastry grid.

Bake the cake in the middle of the oven for about 20 minutes. Remove and leave to cool, then wrap in foil and leave to stand for at least 1 day.

Preparation time:
approx. 40 minutes (plus chilling, baking, cooling and standing time)
Per slice: approx. 530 kcal/2219 kJ

RICOTTA AND FIG CAKE

**Makes 12 slices
(springform tin 26 cm diameter)**

Sponge mixture:
250 g plain flour (patent white)
125 g cold butter
100 g sugar
pinch of salt
1 egg yolk

Topping:
½ vanilla pod
5 figs
2 eggs
100 g icing sugar
500 g ricotta
3 tbsp semolina
pinch of salt
½ cup pine nuts
1 tbsp honey

Additionally:
soft butter for the tin
flour for the work surface

To make the sponge mixture, put the flour in a bowl. Arrange the butter in flakes over the top, then add the sugar, salt and egg yolk. Quickly knead together to make a smooth sponge mix. If it is too dusty, knead in 1–2 tablespoons cold water. Roll out in a ball, then wrap in clingfilm and place in the refrigerator for about 1 hour.

Pre-heat the oven to 180 °C (Gas Mark 4). Butter the springform tin. To make the topping, cut the vanilla pod open with a sharp knife and scoop out the pulp. Wash and dry the figs, then remove the blossom ends and cut the fruits into eighths.

Roll the sponge mixture out on a floured work surface to about 4 cm bigger than the springform tin. Place in the tin, shaping a rim around the edge, and pierce the base several times with a fork. Put the sponge in the refrigerator until required.

Separate the eggs. Using an electric handheld mixer, whisk together the egg yolks, half the icing sugar and the vanilla pulp until creamy. Add the ricotta and the semolina, and stir into the egg yolk mixture with the mixer at the lowest setting. Whisk the egg whites, salt and the remainder of the icing sugar until stiff. Using a wooden spoon, fold one-third of the whisked egg whites into the ricotta mixture, then add the remainder of the egg whites and stir in.

Spread the ricotta mixture over the sponge base and smooth the surface. Arrange the pieces of fig in a circle over the ricotta mixture. Bake the cake in the middle of the oven for about 30 minutes, then leave to cool in the tin. Dry-fry the pine nuts in a pan until golden, then add the honey. Caramelise for about 3 minutes. Spread this mixture over the cake.

Preparation time:
approx. 30 minutes (plus chilling, baking and cooling time)
Per slice: approx. 350 kcal/1465 kJ

SOUTHERN ITALIAN
ORANGE CAKE

Makes 16 slices
(springform tin 26 cm diameter)

Sponge mixture:
220 g flour
salt
50 g sugar
110 g cold butter
1 egg yolk

Topping:
4 non-treated oranges
4 slices candied orange
4 eggs
100 g sugar
2 tbsp orange liqueur
150 ml cream
2–3 tbsp pine nuts

Additionally:
dried legumes to bake blind
icing sugar to dust

Combine all the ingredients to make a smooth sponge mixture, then roll out in a circle. Place the sponge mix in the springform tin and refrigerate for 1 hour.

Wash 2 oranges in hot water and dry. Finely grate the zest. Squeeze out 1 orange. Dice the candied orange slices.

Pre-heat the oven to 180 °C (Gas Mark 4). Cover the sponge mix with baking parchment and weight it down with dried legumes. Bake in the middle of the oven for 10 minutes.

Stir together the eggs, sugar, orange juice and orange liqueur until creamy. Whip the cream until stiff and fold in, together with the grated orange zest and candied oranges. Remove the dried legumes and baking parchment from the pastry. Pour the egg mixture over the sponge mix. Turn the heat down to 160 °C (Gas Mark 1), and bake the cake for 45 minutes until the mixture is set. Leave to cool.

Cut the remaining oranges into segments and arrange over the cake, then sprinkle over the pine nuts and dust with icing sugar. Place the orange cake under the grill for 1–2 minutes until the sugar caramelises.

Preparation time:
approx. 45 minutes (plus chilling, baking and cooling time)
Per slice: approx. 287 kcal/1202 kJ

CROSTATA
DI VISCIOLE

**Makes 16 slices
(springform tin 26 cm diameter)**

400 g sour cherries
300 g sugar
2 cloves
1 cinnamon stick
310 g flour
150 g butter
2 tbsp milk
1 egg
1 egg yolk
pinch of salt

Additionally:
flour for rolling out
butter for the tin
icing sugar to dust
whipping cream to taste

Wash and pit the sour cherries. Then bring to the boil in a saucepan with 150 g sugar, the cloves and the cinnamon, and simmer for about 10 minutes. Remove the cloves and cinnamon.

Combine 1 tablespoon flour with a little cold water, and use to bind the boiling cherries. Leave the cherries to cool.

Quickly make a shortcrust pastry from the remainder of the flour, the butter, the remainder of the sugar, milk, egg, egg yolk and a pinch of salt, then wrap in foil and place in the refrigerator for about 30 minutes. Roll two-thirds of the pastry out on a floured work surface, then butter the springform tin and line with the pastry. Make a rim up the sides. Pre-heat the oven to 175 °C (Gas Mark 3.5).

Spread the thickened cherry mixture over the pastry. Roll out the remainder of the pastry, cut it into squares and arrange over the cherries. Bake the cake in the oven for about 35 minutes. Dust with icing sugar and serve with whipped cream if liked.

Preparation time:
approx. 30 minutes (plus cooking, chilling and baking time)
Per slice: approx. 245 kcal/1026 kJ

TUSCAN
GRAPE BREAD

Makes 10 slices

Yeast dough:
200 ml milk
35 g yeast
150 g sugar
500 g flour
salt
juice and grated zest of
   1 non-treated orange
pulp of 1 vanilla pod
100 g chopped hazelnuts
100 g soft butter
1 egg

Topping:
600 g blue grapes
2 tbsp pine nuts
1 tbsp sugar to sprinkle

Warm the milk, and crumble the yeast into 100 ml milk. Stir in 1 teaspoon sugar. Combine the flour with the remainder of the sugar and the salt. Add the yeast and milk, then cover with flour and leave to rise for 15 minutes.

Combine the orange juice and zest, the vanilla pulp, nuts, butter and egg with the flour, and knead to make a smooth dough. Cover and leave for about 1 hour. Knead the dough well, and shape into a flat bread (1 cm thick). Pre-heat the oven to 180 °C (Gas Mark 4).

Place the bread on a paper-lined baking tray. Wash and pat dry the grapes, then halve them and remove the seeds. Place on the bread with the pine nuts. Sprinkle with sugar and bake in the oven for about 35 minutes. Serve when cool.

Preparation time:
approx. 30 minutes (plus rising,
standing and baking time)
Per slice: approx. 465 kcal/1947 kJ

APPLE PIE
WITH BLACKBERRY SAUCE

Makes 12 slices
(springform tin 24 cm diameter)

320 g flour
170 g coconut oil
120 g butter
¼ tsp salt
6 tbsp ice cold water
1 kg tart apples
1 lemon
150 g sugar
1 tsp cinnamon
¼ tsp grated nutmeg

Blackberry sauce:
300 g fresh blackberries
80 g icing sugar

Additionally:
butter for the tin

Preparation time:
approx. 40 minutes
(plus chilling and baking time)
Per slice: approx. 420 kcal/1758 kJ

In a bowl, combine 300 g flour, the coconut oil, 80 g butter and the salt, either with your hands or with the dough hook of an electric handheld mixer. Gradually add 6 tablespoons ice cold water and continue kneading until the dough is smooth and supple. Dust it with flour, then wrap in aluminium foil and place in the refrigerator for at least 30 minutes.

Peel and quarter the apples, then cut into small pieces and place in a bowl. Squeeze out the lemon and pour 1 tablespoon of juice over the apples; save the rest for later. Season the apples with sugar, cinnamon and nutmeg, and stir in 1 tablespoon of flour.

Pre-heat the oven to 190 °C (Gas Mark 5). Butter the base and sides of the springform tin. Remove the dough from the refrigerator and cut in half. Using a rolling pin, roll out each half in a circle on a floured work surface. Place one circle in the springform tin. Arrange the apple mixture over the top, and dot with 20 g flaked butter. Place the second dough circle on top, trimming any overhanging dough with a knife. Press down around the edges, and dot flakes of the remaining butter over the top. Bake the apple pie in the middle of the oven for about 40 minutes.

Meanwhile, pick over and wash the blackberries for the sauce, and reserve 12 as decoration. Add the remainder of the lemon juice and the icing sugar, and purée with a stick blender. Serve the apple pie from the oven, with the blackberry sauce, and garnish each slice with 1 blackberry.

LIME CAKE
WITH A MERINGUE TOPPING

**Makes 14 slices
(springform tin 24 cm diameter)**

Sponge mixture:

225 g digestive biscuits
125 g butter

Topping:

6 non-treated limes
6 eggs
400 ml sweetened condensed
　milk
2 tbsp cornflour
salt
180 g sugar
big pinch of cream of tartar

Additionally:

butter for the tin

Finely crush the digestive biscuits. The best way to do this is to put the biscuits in a freezer bag and roll over them with a rolling pin until you are left with fine crumbs. Then put in a bowl. Melt the butter in a saucepan and pour over the biscuit crumbs. Combine well. Butter the base and sides of the springform tin. Cover the base of the springform tin with the crumb mixture and press down well. Make a little rim around the sides. Cover and chill for about 30 minutes.

Pre-heat the oven to 180 °C (Gas Mark 4). Wash the limes in hot water and dry, then thinly grate the zest of 3 of them. Squeeze the limes and measure out 125 ml juice.

Separate the eggs. Put the egg whites in the refrigerator. Whisk together the egg yolks and condensed milk until thick and fluffy; this should take at least 5 minutes. Then stir in the lime zest and juice. Sift over the cornflour and whisk until smooth. Pour the cream over the crumb base, and bake in the middle of the oven for about 30 minutes.

Just before the end of the baking time, whisk the egg whites with a little salt until they are fluffy. Slowly whisk in the sugar. Continue whisking until the sugar crystals have dissolved completely and the mixture is stiff.

Finally, whisk in the cream of tartar. Pre-heat the oven to 250 °C (Gas Mark 9). Fetch the pie out of the oven and spoon the meringue mixture over it in clouds. Finish baking on the bottom runner for about 5 minutes, until the peaks of the meringue are nice and brown but not burnt. Leave the pie to cool. Do not refrigerate, and serve on the same day.

Preparation time:
approx. 35 minutes (plus chilling,
baking and cooling time)
Per slice: approx. 350 kcal/1465 kJ

AMERICAN
PINEAPPLE UPSIDE DOWN CAKE

**Makes 12 slices
(springform tin 26 cm diameter)**

Topping:
7 pineapple rings (canned)
60 g soft butter
100 g brown sugar

Sponge mixture:
5 eggs
190 g butter
225 g sugar
pinch of salt
225 g flour

Pre-heat the oven to 175 °C (Gas Mark 3.5). Butter the springform tin. To make the topping, drain the pineapple rings and reserve the juice. Make a light caramel from the butter and brown sugar in a saucepan. Pour into the springform tin, and arrange the pineapple rings on top.

To make the sponge mixture, separate the eggs and whisk the egg whites until stiff. Chill until required. Melt the butter in a shallow saucepan and cool slightly. Cream together the egg yolks, sugar and salt. Stir in the flour, followed by the melted butter and 6 tablespoons of pineapple juice. Fold in the whisked egg whites.

Pour the cake mixture over the pineapple, and bake the cake in the middle of the oven for about 50 minutes. Leave to cool in the tin, then turn out onto a cake plate.

Preparation time:
approx. 35 minutes
(plus baking and cooling time)
Per slice: approx. 382 kcal/1599 kJ

GREENGAGE
UPSIDE DOWN CAKE

**Makes 12 slices
(springform tin 26 cm diameter)**

Topping:
600 g greengages
3 cl vodka
½ tsp jasmine tea

Sponge mixture:
5 eggs
190 g butter
225 g sugar
pinch of salt
225 g flour

To make the topping, wash, halve and stone the greengages. Combine the vodka with the same amount of water. Bring to the boil, and pour over the jasmine tea. Leave to stand for 5 minutes, then strain off the tea and pour over the greengages. Simmer the greengages for at least 20 minutes, then pour off the liquid and drain them.

In the meantime, to make the sponge mixture, separate the eggs and whisk the egg whites until stiff. Chill until required. Melt the butter in a shallow saucepan and cool slightly. Cream together the egg yolks, sugar and salt. Stir in the flour followed by the melted butter. Fold in the whisked egg whites.

Pre-heat the oven to 175 °C (Gas Mark 3.5). Butter a springform tin. Sprinkle the sugar over the base of the tin. Arrange the greengages over the base, then pour over the cake mixture. Bake the cake in the middle of the oven for 50–60 minutes, then leave to cool in the tin. Turn over onto a cake plate to serve.

Preparation time:
approx. 35 minutes
(plus soaking and baking time)
Per slice: approx. 382 kcal/1599 kJ

ORIENTAL
DATE CAKE

Makes 12 slices
(springform tin 26 cm diameter)

400 g fresh dates
150 g almonds
150 g sugar
3 tbsp butter
4 eggs
1 sachet bourbon vanilla sugar
    or the pulp of 1 vanilla pod
3 tbsp cornflour
2 cl orange liqueur

Additionally:
butter for the tin
icing sugar to dust

Pre-heat the oven to 225 °C (Gas Mark 7). Wash and stone the dates, then chop the flesh. Pour boiling water over the almonds and leave to stand for 1 minute. Then pour off the water, and squeeze the almonds to remove the skins.

Place the almonds on a baking tray, and dry them in the oven for about 3 minutes. Cool slightly, then add two-thirds of the sugar and crush in a mortar and pestle or blend in a food processor.

Melt the butter. Separate the eggs. Whisk the egg yolks with the remainder of the sugar and the vanilla sugar or pulp. Stir in the cornflour.

Add the chopped dates, almond mixture, melted butter and orange liqueur to the egg and sugar mixture, and stir carefully. Whisk the egg whites until stiff, and gradually fold into the date mixture.

Butter the springform tin and fill with the date mixture. Bake the cake for 20 minutes, then reduce the temperature to 200 °C (Gas Mark 6) and continue baking for a further 20–25 minutes. Remove from the oven and leave until cold. Dust with icing sugar before serving.

Preparation time:
approx. 20 minutes (plus baking time)
Per slice: approx. 299 kcal/1252 kJ

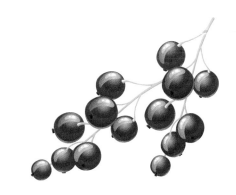

Picture credits

Studio Klaus Arras: p. 19; Klaus Klaussen: p. 75; TLC Fotostudio: all other recipe photos;
Fotolia.com: © Doris Heinrichs p. 6 l, © Africa Studio p. 7 r, © olesyk p. 112 l

Illustrations

Fotolia.com: © Marina Gorskaya